ADOLESCENTS IN SEARCH
OF A NEW CHURCH

ADOLESCENTS IN SEARCH OF A NEW CHURCH

Pierre Babin

Translated and Adapted by
Nancy Hennessy and Carol White

HERDER AND HERDER

1969
HERDER AND HERDER NEW YORK
232 Madison Avenue, New York, N.Y. 10016

Original edition: *L'Eglise,* Editions du Chalet,
Paris, 1968.

Nihil obstat: Leo J. Steady, Censor Librorum
Imprimatur: † Robert F. Joyce, Bishop of Burlington
August 30, 1969

CONTENTS

ADOLESCENTS IN SEARCH
OF A NEW CHURCH

INTRODUCTION

1. *The Church and Young People Today*

An impossible catechesis? Many religion teachers have virtually despaired for several years now of successfully presenting the Church to young people, especially those from sixteen to eighteen. Such a catechesis is considered too abstract, necessarily too doctrinal, too remote from the sensitivities and preoccupation of today's youth. Why?

Two great problems—which seem insurmountable obstacles in a modern context—face religion teachers:

(1) A pedagogical problem of catechetical transmission: how can we translate into the idiom of youth what the Church describes as her own identity?

(2) A more fundamental problem: how can we awaken them to a sense of the Church when the Church itself appears to many as the prime obstacle to their faith?

First problem: catechetical transmission. "When you talk about the Church, you are no longer talking to us. What

11

interested us about this subject is what you told us the first month—when we studied the Church *as seen by the world.* But from there on you lost us with all that stuff about the nature of the Church, the marks of the Church and so on. None of that answers our questions at all!" This comment during a course on the Church summarizes the problem well.

Is it possible that by speaking honestly of the crises and concerns of modern man we can present the Church and the message of Vatican II? Without this, of course, not only shall we fail to interest teenagers, we shall also fail to remain faithful to the Word of God, a Word-made-Flesh, a Word-for-man.

But then how can we go about it? Must we continue to speak of the Church's nature, her structure, her marks? Would that be a *Revelation?* A valid way to reach our contemporaries?

Second problem: the malaise regarding the institutional Church. Here we touch the *basic problem.* It concerns neither the language of catechesis nor the foundation of the Church, Christ. Rather it concerns the Church as an empirical reality, as an institution.[1] Let us start with the facts and attempt a meaningful interpretation of them.

The situation of young people. In sounding out various

[1] This stress upon the malaise regarding the institutional Church does not imply a failure to recognize her mystery. As theologians would express it, to focus upon the institutional aspect of the Church is not to destroy or deny her aspect of mystery. All our efforts with

groups, religion teachers gathered the following typical responses to the questions "How do you see the Church?" and "What are your difficulties?"

—"The Church is an obstacle to freedom; it blocks our growth and expansion."

—"The Church is too much like a domineering mother."

—"The Church is out of another age; it is medieval."

—"*Does* the Church have the truth?"

—"The Church is a moralistic and legalistic institution. There is no significant action for us within the Church. It is irrelevant to us."

—"The Church is tied down too much to the liturgy."

—"The Church isn't Christ; it's a vending machine."

—"It is not God who is dead; it is the Church" (God isn't dead: the Church is, the title of an article in *The Challenge*—January 1967—presenting the results of a survey among teenagers).[2]

Furthermore, beyond questions of language and presentation is the basic issue of the scientific and pluralistic culture which young people face more and more every day and which presents serious questions: Isn't the Church bound to an archaic cultural system? Shouldn't certain forms be replaced by a free, open, and more personal Christian life?

---

students will be directed towards helping them perceive the mystery through and beyond the visible signs.

[2] Although the "death of God" may, for theologians, constitute a more serious problem, it seems to us that this problem concerns a certain elite only. The masses of people are worried about the Church —and not in abstract terms, but concretely, pragmatically.

People are no longer willing to be restricted to membership in some esoteric group. They want to live, as Christians, without that distance from the world imposed by certain rules of worship or disciplines of the Church. We are, before anything else, part of this world and its forward progress. Our faith reveals this world to us; it should not separate us from it. The Church often seems too remote from our way of thinking, feeling, praying, and loving.

Adults. Their view of the problem is somewhat different: depending on their perspective, they reproach the Church with being either too slow or too fast. They will be more upset than teenagers over certain issues of justice, wealth, political involvement, and authoritarian dogmatism. Nonetheless it is significant that among both groups the major problem of faith is clearly the institution of the Church. As A. Savard commented:

As far as God, Christ and the formulation of faith are concerned, answers to a survey reveal a profound religious life fed by modern theology; but this life—despite the strong opposition it encounters in the traditional milieu—can already be classified as "classical."

On the other hand, the question which, in the same survey, concerned the Church, brought answers which in content and form were often vehemently critical: accusations against the hierarchy and the ecclesiastical institution of hypocrisy, false witness, compromise, even "prostitution with all the powers."[3]

[3] In response to a summary of French national meetings on the university parish which appeared in the April 6, 1967 issue of *Le Monde.*

14

These questions, doubts, anxieties seem to refer to the witness given to faith—particularly by the institution—rather than the faith itself.

The Davis case. Take for example the Davis case: Is it not true that this great English theologian caused such a profound stir by his leaving the Church precisely because he united himself with the sufferings and doubts of many others?[4] Admitting that his language and the accents of his own personal crisis are not those of young people, it nonetheless seems to us that he expresses fairly well, in its fundamental impulse, the heart of the malaise:

I remain a Christian, but I have come to see that the Church as it exists and works at present is an obstacle in the lives of the committed Christians I know and admire.

The Church in its existing form seems to me to be a pseudo-political structure from the past. It is now breaking up and some other form of Christian presence in the world is under formation.[5]

The institutional Church is constantly crushing and damaging people. More and more it has become for me a most impersonal, unfree, inhuman system.[6]

[4] "Some events are important in themselves; the import of others is revealed through the echo they call forth in public opinion. The apostasy of the English theologian Davis seems to fall in the second category. Unfortunately it is not unusual for a priest to give up his priesthood and leave the Church. What is unusual is that six months later people are still talking about it. What is exceptional is that the Catholic Press comments on it at length and, on the whole, sympathetically. Even the *Osservatore Romano* discussed it calmly" (I.C.I. No. 285, April 1, 1967, p. 25).

[5] *National Catholic Reporter* (Jan. 4, 1967), p. 7.

[6] *National Catholic Reporter* (Jan. 25, 1967), p. 6.

It is obvious that the basic problem here is the empirical structure of the Church, particularly the "monarchical" quality of the structure, with all that that implies for the conception of freedom, of transmission of doctrine, and human relations. Can Christ and "fullness of life" be given us today in this structure? Must we not find them elsewhere, and in another manner?

An explanation. After having described the environment, let us come back to the young people themselves. Can their youth, as well as the time and the world in which they live, furnish us an explanation of their malaise, that is to say, of their estrangement from the Church?

We are old in the Church. When the young people tell us, "Christ, yes, the Church, no," that is, "The reality, yes, the sign, no," we must in the first place realize that they speak to us with the truthfulness and grace of youth. Part of the grace of youth is going to the essential, and rejecting superstructures and false rationalizations.

Perhaps even at the age of 25 we are already old in the Church, used to genuflections and the liturgy. They are young: as they leave childhood behind they see the Church with new eyes. Thanks to the absolute and impatient quality of their age they stumble, more than we do, over the slowness and historical deformations, over the heaviness and

16

practical realism of the age. They compare the world which moves and the Church which lasts, the bright lights of the city and the dimness of the church built of stone. If they object, or look the other way, it is first of all because this is their first look, a look which seeks the absolute and success. Of course they already knew the Church in the world of their childhood; but they knew it with the knowledge of their parents, the knowledge of a now distant world, a world which they have perhaps rejected. Now, for the first time, they look at the Church by themselves, asking basic questions: "Is this where we find life? Is this where things happen?"

Let us not be surprised at the hardness of their look and of their criticism. It is, no doubt, suffering for us, but for them it is grace, a kind of evangelical grace. Half the new generation always has the role of renewing things by returning to essentials. How could a teacher who does not recognize this grace, does not welcome the impatient and deep desires of today's youth, speak of the Council, of the Incarnation, and of the Aggiornamento?

Two main lines of reaction. Now that young people are awakening to the quality of their personal lives, the Church confronts them as a reality to which they are bound but within which they do not really belong. What is their reaction, their first thoughtful and personal response?

Of various types of response, ranging from the rebellious

to the reactionary, two groups stand out among those with whom we have most contact. We usually find them side by side in religion classes:

(1) A majority of the indifferent;

(2) An elite of those we might call "uneasy" about religion.

The indifferent. For these—and they are numerous—the Church is simply dull, slightly "boring." They say this without antagonism, without aggression. They have not suffered greatly from rigid structures at home or in school; they are free from bitterness; they are even willing to admit that, since the Council, the Church has progressed. But essentially none of this matters.

Their attitude is not so much scandalized revolt from the institution of the Church as calm detachment from it and its dogmatic, liturgical, and moral formulas. Why? Because their lives are busy, because they are affected by the barrage of the mass media, and because they do not suffer from a burdensome religious super-ego. They have no reason to resent the Church and little desire even to reproach it with its own irrelevance. The Church is simply not "with it." Although they may continue to believe vaguely in God and perhaps even work courageously towards building the City of Man, there is no question of their fighting over the liturgy or over permission to use the pill. They'll *manage,* that's all.

If these young people are indifferent to the Church, they are not indifferent to a human existence which has quality. Many have discovered that one can have high moral standards, sound ethical principles, and authentic freedom without necessarily belonging to the Church. As one girl claimed upon returning from a summer project with disadvantaged children: "There we *lived*. We had great discussions and tremendous freedom. So what's the point of being Christian?" Which is to say "What is the point of belonging to a Church with all its battery of laws in order to be happy, to live well, to work?"

The uneasy ones. For these the Church is simultaneously fascinating because of the gospel she mysteriously reveals and repulsive because of her external forms, her archaic language, and her artificial relationships.

They care about God, prayer, spiritual realities, but they cannot connect what the Church presents with what they themselves experience within the world as true and good and vital. Thus they claim, "The rites and laws of the Church no longer fulfill our need for authenticity." During a recent CCD weekend some of the students, after an earnest attempt to participate in the Eucharist, approached the priest: "It's no use, Father, it just doesn't make that much sense. There's no link between our real concerns and the liturgy. You might as well have left it in Latin."

Examples are legion; underneath them all is the same

fundamental criticism: the institution is inadequate. It does not help us to pray; it does not help us to live; it does not give us freedom. It is, in fact, in our way.

We must realize that these young people, educated in the modern sciences, have developed a mental structure that is concrete, demanding, critical. Whatever they cannot verify, experience, or feel as good and valid, they will no longer continue to accept as right and true. They speak, furthermore, with the calm assurance that flows from a collective and irreversible experience of the values of the human person, of his intelligence, and of his freedom. Yves Madonet characterizes this quest for authenticity and experiential truth as follows:

For them truth is no longer ready-made, as unchangeable as an ancient document. It is a truth to be created . . . It has become pragmatic. The good and the true is that which works, which can be verified, which succeeds. The truth of moral, religious or philosophical doctrines is no longer determined by logical criteria. Rather it is judged by what they bring to concrete, real life. *Lived experience becomes the great criterion of value.* They no longer bother with codes or written counsels. Only one question counts: "If I try it, will it succeed?"[7]

Caught in this tension between personal experience and the traditional forms of the Church, their deep religious spirit is in search, hesitating between criticism and rejection. The best among them, in the depths of their being, desire above all to be affirmed as free to search, without at the

[7] *Presse-Actualité.* 33 (March 1967), p. 55.

same time being reprimanded by the Church: to live as Christians without belonging to a caste.

2. Should We Be Pessimists?

The possibilities. Our description of those uneasy about religion hints enough at the secret aspirations of young people for us to be pessimistic, to despair of catechesis. We must admit these aspirations without letting difficulties conceal possibilities. Their expectation seems to be rooted in a longing for depth, solidity, and total openness. From their initiation, with puberty, into the subjective conflicts of adolescence, they have an inarticulate desire for concrete foundations and realistic goals in their lives. Still anesthetized by mass culture and excited by the drive for success, they have an increasingly tangible and fierce need to *go further,* to live and love for good. Hippies or not, they long for friendship, communication, meaning, and participation in actions which are worthwhile and which make them more human.

It is within this void that there appears—paradoxical as it may seem—the image of and a vague need for the Church: as a place of participation, a center for wholeness and totality.

"How can we understand this world and the style to which it is being born? Which group offers meaning, solutions, full realization of my desire to participate? Is the truth located in this Church into which I was born? Shall I make my life here?" Such are their profound expectations and genuine questions.

Our premises. In light of this description, positive as well as negative, two convictions appear:

(1) Despite all the difficulties, a healthy understanding of the psycho-sociology of modern youth leads us to the conclusion that it is possible for them to reflect upon the Church. Such reflection helps them consciously to accept or refuse this Church which was given them in childhood, which claims to offer special meanings and powers, an interpretation of the world as grounded in Christ, and the attraction of the fullness of life.

(2) Nonetheless, a catechesis of the Church for young people today requires:

—new emphases in the doctrinal presentation;

—a profound renewal in pedagogical attitudes and catechetical methods.

For the catechetical formula: "This is what you must believe," we must substitute the invitation: "Let us seek faith together." Only in the freedom of a group search will young people be able to discover personally *their* Church which is the Church of Christ.

3. *Our Quest*

The main lines. The catechetical method itself calls for an initial reflection: The major influence on catechesis of the

Church seems to be the cultural change currently transforming various structures of thinking, seeing, and learning among young people. The transition to a pluralistic society demands new ways of learning and new requirements for the proposition of faith. This will be dealt with initially.

A second reflection will deal with questions of the doctrinal and spiritual emphases of this catechesis of the Church.[8]

The spirit: Vatican II? People have asked us what we are doing with the Council. That Vatican II—as the major event for interpreting our times and the Christian spirit within them—is at the heart of the document *The Church and the Modern World* is evident enough. The Council is indeed to some extent "the great light." But this does not mean we must set its message up as the goal students must reach ("Sit still and learn") or as the ultimate formula ("Here is the absolute truth; there is nothing more for you to seek").

[8] It is therefore evident that the reflections which follow must go beyond the simple problem of catechesis to investigate this problem in its context of a modern, scientific, democratic, and pluralistic society. And yet, we must guard against setting up as absolute or definitive what is proposed here. We shall continually endeavor to remember:

—that pluralism does not actually exist in every milieu or in every country and that consequently our reflections must remain relative and partial;

—that our concern here is with late adolescents and not younger teenagers (between thirteen and fifteen). The key import of these pages is to help us discern the direction our efforts should take and the type of new man—of modern Christian—whom we hope to educate.

Merely to talk about or "rehash" the Council would be to demonstrate that it is dead. Proof that the Council is truly *Spirit* and *Life* resides in our recreating it, or better still, in our assisting young people themselves to recreate it, to give it room to grow through their own capacities for understanding and experience.

Why isn't it sufficient to talk about the Council? Not only because of the young people themselves, but even more significantly because the Word of God itself is obliged to be in immediate contact with the concerns and mental habits of modern youth; because the Word of God desires, here and now, to become flesh, that is, to be spoken with the accents, sensitivities, and inflections of today's young people.

Our work is not theological systematization; it is pastoral, prophetic, and charismatic. Woe to him who merely copies and rehashes: he betrays the Incarnation and redemption. The document *The Church and the Modern World* attempts to recreate. This effort is not normative but meaningful and stimulating. Finally it seeks to propose a method better designed to educate a Christian who is free, loving, open, and true to the evolution demanded by this age and called forth by the Holy Spirit.

PART ONE

THE SITUATION

Cultural Change

THE SITUATION

Significant facts. In a recent issue of *Playboy* a thirteen-page article on the Church by Harvey Cox was sandwiched between the Playmate of the Month, the Vargas cartoon, and various other articles and ads which had, to say the least, nothing to do with traditional morality (Gentlemen, take your choice!).

During a discussion of the vocation of women among seniors in a Catholic girls' high school, the following question was put to the speaker: "Is there any really *good* reason for virginity before marriage now that we have the pill?"

Each of us could provide thousands of such instances. What is happening?

The key problem. Essentially it is this: Modes of thought and life, filtered and directed by an authoritarian, self-enclosed educational system, were formerly the same for all young people. Today these modes are much more flexible and suggest, outside of any authoritarian context, a thousand

27

ways of belief, of success, and of commitment. Sexual behavior, Church membership, vocational selection all become open, matters of choice and not of tradition.

We should, therefore, focus our attention upon this situation of cultural pluralism or polyculture. In general the one event which most affects the issue of faith for young people today, and therefore their education, is this transition from a traditional or authoritarian society to a pluralistic one.[9]

Therefore, for an understanding of and catechesis of the Church, pluralism is all the more significant. Indeed the Church, more than any other reality of faith, presents itself to us as a cultural and historical manifestation. If God and Christ retain, somewhat spontaneously in the eyes of the world, a certain transcendence, the Church does not; her human face confronts us from the start. Thereby, more so than other realities of faith, it risks being discredited or considered simply as one cultural system among many, one moreover which appears out of date.

If cultural pluralism does indeed constitute the heart of the question, it must be analyzed more closely. It is no exaggeration to say that this new social structure must lead to a new kind of education and therefore, for us, a new kind of catechetical transmission.

[9] No doubt we should also discuss the industrial context or the technological, urban, social, and international context. But—apart from the fact that their consequences for faith have already been frequently studied—it seems to us that the import of cultural pluralism encompasses and informs all other modern realities and constitutes the concrete fact by which these young people experience these other realities.

I.

CULTURE AND THE QUEST FOR MEANING

1. *What Is Culture?*

In order to understand properly the new issue of faith provoked by pluralism we must consider certain preliminary notions concerning "culture" and its influence on existence.

Culture, as explored by Friedman, can be defined rather broadly as the "sum total of efforts" which take place within a given community in order to solve the problem of existence.[10]

A fork, a handshake, the mass media, central heating, poetry, feasts, language: all are attempts to solve the problem of existence. Imagine, for example, the tremendous effort expended by culture in a northern country to develop fat, sweet foods, storm windows, and whole systems which make the interiors of houses comfortable. Or note the ways in which men have fought against the night: electric lights; the feast of Christmas which during the darkest period of the year celebrates "the day star on high." Note too how men have struggled against aging and the change of seasons by growing fir trees and evergreens, the only plants which

---

[10] G. Friedman, "Le pluralisme due point de vue de l'anthropologie culturelle," *Table Ronde* 226 (Nov. 1966), pp. 41 and 59. We shall refer frequently to this article, without entering the debate among sociologists and humanists, because the issues he raises correspond with our own approach.

do not lose their leaves, and which therefore proclaim a victory over decay. Culture is thus the fruit and expression of a group's common reaction to a given situation, a problem they must attempt to solve.

One hardly need stress that culture so conceived is not merely some external atmosphere in which men live as sponges in water and which they could perhaps escape. Culture penetrates much deeper than that: it is as much part of our vital impulse and effort as the society in which we live. The current generation of teenagers participates actively in the play of interrelationships, in resolving existential problems and therefore, in creating and bending culture in a new direction.

2. *Two Great Needs That Must Be Solved*

What characterizes a human culture? In every human culture two kinds of need must be fulfilled: material needs which we share with animals—food, shelter, reproduction—and specifically human, spiritual needs. Basically every culture tries to satisfy a need for meaning; it tends to provide a universal system of explanations and solutions. Even mass culture, however much we deplore its worldly pragmatism, does not escape this law. As Morin defines it:

A culture constitutes a complex body of norms, symbols, myths, and images which penetrate the individual's privacy, structure his insights and condition his emotions. A culture provides imaginary points of support for practical living and practical points of support

30

for imaginary life; it nourishes the half-real, half-imaginary being which each man produces in his soul, the half-real, half-imaginary being which each man constructs outside himself and with which he surrounds himself.[11]

We need only read the advice of columnists like Ann Landers, sanctioned by the "common sense" of vast audiences, to note the pretensions of mass culture to furnish a system of universals, solutions highly precarious as far as deeper meanings go. Culture, in other words, seeks to satisfy the specifically human need to discover a meaning in life which is coherent and justified. What is man? Where is he going? What is his purpose in life? What is the meaning of the love and drive for power at the heart of human existence?

Because we in a sense are specialists in questions of meaning, the answers to these eternal questions are of the keenest interest to us—which is not to say that Christians are the only such specialists. Philosophers, believers or not, are also preoccupied with these questions, but Christians are specialists in an ultimate sense. In any case, contrary to common expectation, satisfaction of the need for meaning does not occur only in the form of intellectual research. The average man does not ask such general questions as "What is life all about?" Rather the more we move into a secular civilization, the less, according to Harvey Cox, men ask abstract questions about death and human destiny. Modern man is pragmatic; he seeks solutions for precise and concrete problems. Thus, those questions that constitute the fine points of

[11] *L'Esprit du Temps,* p. 12, Paris.

catechesis are no longer valid. Does this mean that we will no longer be men who, in the name of faith, "arouse anxiety" by probing the problems of meaning? No, we shall continue, but in a new way.

3. *How Does Man Satisfy His Need for Meaning?*

According to sociologists, every man, whatever his age or location, first fulfills his need for meaning, not theoretically but through a concrete search in two complementary directions: the quest for identity and the quest for participation. *The quest for identity* expresses itself in the need for recognition, for acceptance, for affirmation of oneself. One wants, that is, to be someone to others, someone who is desired if not needed. With this desire satisfied one can achieve a fulfillment of one's self image which concretizes the meaning of one's existence. Conversely the person no one listens to, no one desires, tends to lose a grip on the meaning of his life. *The quest for participation* is the quest for action and creativity which is both meaningful in regard to the total movement of the group, the society or the world, and satisfactory in regard to personal fulfillment. It means placing one's own tiny block into the building of the world or into the highway of history, a stone that is small but nonetheless necessary and important. Any expression—belonging to a union, supporting a family, working in a political campaign, participating in a movement—can be seen as a contribution to the improvement of society. It is clear that in this expression of self, through this creation and this sharing, man finds an inherent meaning in life. The man who lacks this —who feels himself excluded, unrecognized, without potential for useful action or social participation—can find no meaning in life.

Satisfying the need for meaning thus appears linked primarily to the concrete conditions of all human existence rather than to abstract questioning. And it is at this level that we should first respond.

4. *Modern Culture Differs from Traditional Culture*

There is no doubt that modern culture—even mass culture —satisfies at least in part this continual human quest for identity and participation. The deluge of response to radio call-in programs or letters-to-the-editor columns reveals the general need to be recognized and to have something to say to others.

And yet one thing radically distinguishes modern pluralism from traditional culture—the very method of solving questions of meaning.[12] Here we touch the heart of the issue. Briefly, young people in traditional cultures generally had no option among several possibilities: they were not able to choose their modes of identity and of participation.

[12] We shall, to be explicit, contrast traditional society and modern pluralism, recognizing that there exists another type between these two, the "inner-directed" in Riesman's terms.

Today, on the other hand, almost everything presents an option, with several alternatives. This change is of fundamental importance in regard to the problematic and education of faith. Let us analyze it further.

II.

THE PROBLEMATIC AND EDUCATION OF FAITH IN TRADITIONAL SOCIETIES

How was the question of a search for meaning posed in traditional societies—if indeed it was asked at all? We can schematize it under two points:

(1) *The meaning was not chosen from among other possible meanings.*

According to the proverb, one's country determines one's religion. When an ancient ruler was baptized, his whole country became Christian.

The child born in a traditional rural village does not choose his faith, his meaning of life from among several options. A village in Corsica, surrounded by walls, suspicious of "strangers" from the next village, and ingrown, possesses a whole system of formulas, customs, relationships, feasts, and songs. The child born there is automatically acculturated into the only existing society, the village, which is omnipresent, fully explained, and guaranteed by mayor, teacher, priest, and the old folk of the countryside.

What happens when this child becomes fifteen? There is no question of his *choosing* his faith or his morality. The seventeen-year-old girl who ventures out into the village streets with a boy is pointed at by all and immediately becomes the subject of gossip. What can she do? Social pressure is such that no discussion is possible: she must either exile herself or accept the canon of customs which forbids this relationship. Choice does not mean in this case selecting from among various options within the culture, but rather conforming to the group or being excluded from it. And the price of exclusion is so costly that only very strong persons are willing to pay it!

Even within the culture the quest for identity and participation and consequently for meaning is not a matter of choice; it is established by birth and by custom. In some places the "little hunchback" automatically became a tailor or cobbler; the oldest son succeeded his father; and large families had to produce at least one priest and one soldier. The child could "choose"—not to do something else, but—to make the most of this situation and to find within it the meaning of his life.[13]

(2) *Religious meanings were intimately linked to the realities of daily life.*

In other words, in a traditional society culture was monolithic. Material and spiritual realities, action and meaning were intimately united, and the fulfillment of everyday needs went hand in hand with transcendentals. Consider, for in-

[13] Fourastie describes the traditional atmosphere well; he notes in particular that the elements of traditional morality are those which maintain, conserve, and provide for the continuity of a closed, fixed order. "The basic social rule is succession . . . Thus the laborer is the son of a laborer, the master son of a master, the count son of a count, and the emperor son of an emperor" (*Essais de Morale Prospective* [Paris, 1966], pp. 11–57).

stance, ancient village feasts which featured pigeon shooting, high Mass, laying wreaths upon graves, dancing, vespers, a fair. Another example is the custom in private schools of beginning and ending each class with a prayer, a ritual which is, at the same time, a time signal, an act of discipline, and a religious act.

Thus the "religious" and the "eating-drinking-sleeping" spheres were part of culture without clearly marked distinctions. The bell for recreation was called "the voice of God." Everything was mixed together without people being aware of it.[14]

CONSEQUENCES

1. *The Problematic of Faith*

In a traditional village a girl in charge of fellow adolescents told the priest: "When you speak to the girls about conscience and personal prayer, I'm not sure how much they get out of it. They go to Mass but they don't really experience personal prayer—a reflective, individual act; they participate in the singing, they are there, they follow the prescribed ritual—and that's all."

This girl had gone a step ahead of her friends, a step of which she was painfully aware. Under the pressures of external events and cultural change, she had been forced to

[14] As Fourastie notes, quite rightly, in a traditional society "morality and religion are also ways of making use of time" (*op. cit.,* p. 29).

choose her faith—that is, to reflect upon it, and to compare it with other systems. As a result she was fully aware of the difference which separated her from the others: for them, faith and the meaning given to life constituted neither a problem nor an option. They were globally and unconsciously Christian.[15]

Hence to speak of the "problem of faith" is to refer to a problem which doesn't exist. The only problem would arise from the extent of one's participation, as he grows up, within the group (if that involvement conflicts with his own subjective needs). This is a problem of fervor or intensity, not one of doubt. Many will admit, "We believe, but we don't practice because there's no time for it."[16]

2. *The Education of Faith*

The key to the education of faith in this traditional culture was the *catechism*. If, today, we have so much trouble agreeing on a catechism, the prime reason is that we are in the

[15] "Unconscious" is used here in a broad sense to mark the absence of reflective awareness or better still, in the words of Sartre, the absence of "positional consciousness." They had none of that detachment which enables one to question the assumptions of his given world.

[16] Actually this situation in most countries has generally disappeared. Most young people find themselves in the middle position between traditional and pluralistic cultures. *Crisis of Faith* (Pierre Babin, New York, 1963) analyzes this in-between situation, describing the three kinds of conversion thus possible for those from seventeen to twenty-four.

midst of this crisis of cultural change: it is no longer possible to educate in the old way.

Three statements can be made about the function of the catechism in traditional cultures:

(1) It was primarily for *children*—that is, for people who would not argue back. Learning was strictly a matter of obedience and rote memorization.

(2) It represented a synthesis of acculturation: a grammar of the world, a system of interpretation, a code of conduct and a solution of life's problems.

(3) It presupposed a whole social environment which guaranteed its effectiveness. One didn't go to catechism class just to learn but also to become, under group pressure, "a nice little child," who would eventually receive his first holy communion.[17] It has been observed that at the very moment the family or social environment failed—the moment when other cultures invaded the realm of the mother culture—the crisis of the catechism began.

What about adolescents? Could their religious education be the object of research and study in such a context? Obviously not. Educating adolescents in faith simply meant a continuation along the lines of the catechism: dogmatic, didactic instruction conceived as an advanced catechism or an abbreviation of systematic theology. If the young person

---

[17] See J. A. Dhotel, S.J., *The Origins of the Modern Catechism* (Paris, 1966). The author explicates the pastoral preoccupations of the catechism: ". . . the primacy given to religious instruction against errors, against ignorance . . . and the loosening of morals" (pp. 12–13).

had doubts—due to psychological difficulties or libertine rationalizations—he was administered a sound apologetic designed to guarantee once and for all that his faith would be solid. This was sufficient in traditional cultures because these doubts rose not from hesitation when confronted with various options but from subjective struggles. Furthermore, only well-developed personalities were open to such doubts.

Belief therefore was translated into conditions of obedience, resignation, and fidelity—which did not, incidentally, exclude the possibility of freedom or joy. The rule given by St. Francis de Sales to Christians of his time was handed on (in religious communities) for centuries: "Ask nothing; refuse nothing." And this could be a great form of holiness in traditional societies. But who today, in our country at least, could really live in freedom without a faith which has been chosen and thoroughly reflected upon, or without a commitment sought and accepted along quite different paths?

III.

THE PROBLEMATIC AND EDUCATION OF FAITH
IN PLURALISTIC SOCIETIES

Have I chosen the right way? Fifteen-year-old John has grown up in a religious but open family·which brought neither strong pressures nor stifling controls to bear on him. He voluntarily attends religion class in his high school. He reads best-sellers, watches TV, participates regularly in the activities of a teen club, goes camping in the summer and skiing with friends in the winter. What problems of faith could John have?

John does not seem to be rebelling against the faith of the Church or of his parents. Riesman's analysis of the other-directed type suggests that such aggression is no longer current among young people. Their problem is not violence but indifference.[18] And even if John is not indifferent, his problem is not to resist past formation but to evaluate future possibilities and choose one. Is it along this line that I shall find truth and love? (Think of the film *The Graduate.*)

Because pluralism profoundly influences the classical issue of faith, it also affects the education of faith.

---

[18] This is not to say that within more traditional families where a strong ideology prevails, young people are not more strongly marked as reactionary or rebellious. This emphasizes again the tentative nature of our analysis.

1. *The Problematic of Faith*

To find meaning is a problem of choice: pluralism and the need to choose. The search for identity and participation today is no longer assured by birth or by custom; it is a problem of having to choose from among a thousand possible solutions. This is the condition imposed by pluralism which consists precisely in the fact that within a society there coexist without conflict various ways of satisfying these needs.

Whereas formerly in rural areas the eldest son, having finished school, carried on his father's work, today the widest diversity of vocations is open to him. Thus the young person, having left behind the strong social pressures of a traditional society, faces a new problem. Although nearly unlimited possibilities are open to him from which he can construct a physical and spiritual focus for his life, he lacks the norms with which to direct such a choice.

The problem of faith. Faith can be considered by psychosociologists as one more variant in the general search for meaning. How is this question posed?

Whereas in traditional societies there was no crisis, no questioning, in authoritarian cultures (the bourgeois society at the turn of this century for example) faith became a problem: not one of choosing among several religions all equally

42

available but one of questioning, of reacting against the education received from parents. What is the situation today in a pluralistic society? Is faith a problem? Not necessarily. What does constitute a problem—an acute and explicit problem—is the quest for meaning. No one, insofar as he is human, can escape this problem. But in the posing of this question, faith is not necessarily included. It is possible for us to solve it quite adequately without even touching the issue of faith.

I am able to give meaning to my life without faith. Under what conditions does faith appear as a problem? First and foremost, if young people have been touched by the signs of Christ—through a meeting with a priest, education at home, reading the gospel, a religious program on TV, whatever; the roads vary greatly. In any case, it is certain that faith will in no way form part of the problem of meaning if the

· young person has not experienced in some way the active presence and word of Christ. In this light, is faith today sufficiently proclaimed? Does it reach young peoples' awareness in all its dimensions?

Secondly, the problem of faith is subjectively all the sharper today because of the demands by young people for solutions which have depth, genuineness, and experiential validity. This insistence is common among all young people whatever their background—not just Christian. They are dissatisfied with the poverty in human relationships and worried about finitude and relativism, that is, about the inconsistencies of their experience. Many would agree with Morin's stress, in the conclusion of his study of mass culture, that this culture poses a basic problem, that of significance and immortality.[19]

Certainly many boys and girls are too demanding interiorly to be satisfied indefinitely with the easy answers of the mass media or the apparent promiscuity of *Playboy*.[20]

Faith demands a choice. Inasmuch as one can survive quite well in total indifference or without recognizing its signs, faith is not necessarily a problem. But it is a problem for the young person solicited both by faith and by other options, who can no longer commit himself to Christian life without having first discussed, reflected upon, and finally *chosen* it.

This is certainly one of the newest aspects of the issue of faith today. From an external, cultural perspective, Christian life no longer appears as THE solution but as ONE solution. It is no longer social or parental pressure which leads to faith but personal evaluation and the choice of a specific group.[21]

[19] *L'Esprit du Temps,* pp. 239 ff., Paris.

[20] Ultimately a lack of morality and belief leads to boredom rather than to freedom. This is one reason to agree with Giroud that modern society is heading for an enthusiasm . . . for transcendence . . . or at least for the spiritual (*Inter-Club* [Feb. 1967], p. 90).

[21] It goes without saying that this whole analysis is made from an external viewpoint. The Christian knows that every road has its primary source in the call of God and is effected in grace.

Belonging to a religious group becomes necessary for a vision of faith. Another characteristic of modern societies is that they no longer impose a monolithic vision of the world, essentially because, having turned towards utilitarian ends, they are marked by science and technology. Science inherently rejects systematic explanation—this is the reason for its success. Since science is concerned with solving specific, clearly determined problems, to live in a technological age with a grand, all-encompassing vision of the world is impossible.

What solution, then, remains for the one who feels the need for a general explanation? According to Friedman, the solution seems to consist "in the formation of voluntary communities with primarily ethical and religious motivations, communities in which the individual offers no resistance whatsoever to what seeks to reveal itself in and to him. The voluntary community with the practical-ethical tasks it assigns itself is the new form of 'universe,' grasped at a glance, which corresponds to the person's efforts to attain to totality."[22]

Is this not relevant to the problem of the Church and of Christian community? Oddly enough, culturally speaking, the Church in the etymological sense of "assembly" will become more necessary than ever. But, at the same time—and herein lies the difficulty—young people will become increasingly demanding about belonging to this Church: they will compare it with other groups; they will choose it; they will

[22] *La Table Ronde* 226 (Nov. 1966), p. 45.

hope to find within it a climate of search for total meaning according to Christ, rather than a direction for their actions.

Summary. Faith has become the object of personal evaluation, a choice from among several options. Any total vision of the world requires, furthermore, the choice of a specific ethical or religious group which is distinct from the secularized society in which we live.

2. *The Education of Faith*

In such a context, with such a problem, what are the new requirements for catechesis and religious education? Because the next chapters will attempt to reply precisely and concretely to answer this question with specific orientation and methods, our reply here will be brief. It is, moreover, too soon to discern exactly how the transmission of faith will be marked by the cultural change we are now experiencing.

Briefly therefore: knowing *how to choose* will become more important than simply knowing. No doubt a certain basic knowledge will always be needed, but it is impossible today to know all one ought to know, and, furthermore, given the acceleration of progress, it is difficult to accept as definitive and permanent any formula of knowledge.

Formerly in the education of faith the task was to transmit effectively and to make people learn well, by guaranteeing maximum group membership and traditional truth. This truth was above discussion.

Today education should be concerned first of all with teaching young people how to see, then to evaluate, and finally to choose. Since all formulas for faith and life are open to them, the question of our determining the content of their belief and action no longer exists. The question rather is one first of educating them to *recognize* what is good and true.

A sixteen-year-old told his catechetics teacher: "You say that premarital sex relations are wrong, that they are forbidden. But that's your opinion. Other people have different ideas. Once we have experimented with it, if it hurts us, we'll admit it's wrong. Until then why should we believe you?"

The same sort of reasoning could be given for belonging to the Church. Perception, evaluation, choice: such, it seems, should be the objective of an education of faith for youth. And in a pluralistic world, this presumes that the Word of the Lord and the life of the Church be proclaimed with greater concern for freedom and integrity than ever before.

PART TWO

THE OBJECTIVES

THE OBJECTIVES

In light of these cultural changes, what should our objectives be in educating young people to believe in the Church? Each teacher must, of course, decide for himself about concrete goals suited to his own group and to his own gifts. But more generally we can explore certain global objectives shaped by our intuitions of an emerging society:

(1) to educate for norms of choice and for voluntary community;

(2) to educate for the experience of love;

(3) to educate for dialogue and solidarity with all men;

(4) to educate for a sense of mission.

Although the first objective is no more important than the others, it will be developed more fully because it is the newest and the most problematic in a pluralistic society.

As we have said, we must anticipate and form a new type of man arising from this new society: Christian, deeply attached to the Lord and his Church but quite detached from traditional structures, freely choosing to pursue the truth continually revised by experience. This educational task is an urgent one.

I.

FIRST OBJECTIVE:
NORMS OF CHOICE AND
VOLUNTARY COMMUNITY

The objective of educating young people to choose—one stressed most recently in pedagogical circles—follows directly from an analysis of pluralism. The young person breaking from the cocoon of his home environment is suddenly solicited by everything. He will instinctively try out many things, experience sorrow and elation, investigate the pros and cons of dreams of success offered by both Church and country club, by sports, girls, and money. His first acculturation was unconscious; his adjustment now must be motivated by choice. Adolescence means reaching this stage of choice. This suggests how important it is to form in adolescents, not traditionally but pluralistically, the capacity to evaluate and choose among several alternative life styles.

The heart of the question: the norms of choice. But how do we educate for this? How can we assure that the Church as a voluntary, meaningful community, is acknowledged, reflected upon, and chosen in full consciousness and freedom without the pressure of traditional monolithic directives? What will permit young people to recognize among the proposed alternatives the Good and the True and to choose the community which opens out onto the highest meanings?

A general theory. By accepting the perspective of the very people we are attempting to educate, we can evolve a general theory of formation. This theory can then be concretized in practical terms.

WHAT ARE SOME POSSIBLE NORMS?

Listen to the young people:

"Why should I confess my sins to some strange priest? That kind of legalistic ritual has nothing whatsoever to do with my life. Confession might be real if I admitted my error to the people I live with and was forgiven and helped by the people around me. If the priest were a member of this group, then the absolution I received from him might be authentic. But I don't want it the other way: huddled alone in some dark corner beating my breast for my own private relief."

"You tell us that Christ is Truth, the meaning of life. But how do we know that? I certainly don't see it or feel it—I don't hear his voice, that's for sure—and I can't pretend that I know it if I don't. I've got to be true to myself."

"It's no use labeling things as right or wrong until we've tried them out first, and even then each person has to discover what is good or bad for himself. If I experience something as destructive for me, then I'll avoid it. If I experience it as positive—that goes for pot, sex, dropping out of school —I'll choose it, no matter what the authorities say."

These statements reveal clearly that the criterion of choice for young people today is experience.

The experience of value. Typically young people recognize a reality as true and good because they experience it as a value for them, as meaningful in their own lives, as fulfilling. As soon as they experience this as good for themselves and others, they tend to identify it as "good." What seems good to them now tends to become "absolutely good," and they pass imperceptibly from the experiential value, good-for-me, good-for-us, to the good-in-itself. Thus the passage to the transcendental or absolute takes place through their concrete experience of value.

Whereas traditional recognition of good and evil, true and false, took place unconsciously through participation in the clan, young people today demand a personal conscious experience, profound and discriminating. Not only is this conscious personal dimension already an accomplished fact on the practical level of life, men also desire it for deeper realities. They will no longer tolerate functioning like IBM computers whose every action is programmed. They want to take the most momentous decisions into their own hands.

Is this true of faith as well? Yes, certainly, if we agree about our assumptions.

The heart of the question. The experience of value can be a norm in the choice of faith if we admit that God is the ultimate horizon, always distinct but not always evident in all we think, love and desire. As St. Thomas said, man is open to God because he is open to being. In other words, every experience of value is unconsciously an experience of God and constitutes what Rahner calls "anonymous Christianity." Although its explicit translation would require a revelation, the experience of value already forms the threshold of the sanctuary of absolute mystery.[23]

Such was the experience of St. Augustine who in his quest for truth and love, however imperfect, was living unconsciously in the realm of Truth and Love; although the light of goodness which he ardently pursued was not the full light, it was already an approach to, a remote participation in the Light.

Whatever road you have traveled, do not stop; always go further. Follow your light even if it is only a dim ray; protect your flame even if it is weak. Call the Mystery to you for the very reason that it escapes you. Go on and you will discover; hope with certainty that your hope has already in the depth of your being received its accomplishment.[24]

---

[23] Karl Rahner in "Is Faith Possible Today?" thus states that Christianity is nothing else than the experience of this transcendence, provided that we do not cheapen this experience or fail to follow it through.

[24] Rahner, *op. cit.,* p. 54.

The experience of value can thus be considered the norm in the decision for faith[25] provided we persevere to the end: God is the horizon and foundation of all value. But we must be clear on several points.

1. The Concept of Value

Following Berger's guideline[26] we can define value as, simultaneously, a reality tested by experience and a reality recognized as value. This formulation provides a perspective on the absolute: "Value exists only through and for the subject who *experiences* it through an act that we call appreciation, and *recognizes* it as opening out to the Absolute." "Value is felt as a transcendental call: . . . it presents itself not as one's own achievement but as originating outside the self."

2. The Special Character of the Experience of Faith

All men are not called, here and now, to the experience of the True and Good revealed by the Church. A special grace from the Lord is needed: "No one knows the Father but the Son, and he to whom the Son wishes to reveal Him."

The experience of the Church's life as value is not in

[25] Cf. Mouroux, *Christian Experience,* New York, 1956.
[26] G. Berger in "Modern Man and His Education," *PUF,* pp. 327–328.

itself completely irresistible. Nor is it essential. It originates in the free design of God. This partially explains why many young people, though physically baptized, are not open to the mysterious sign of the Church.[27]

3. *The Word Is Needed to Reveal the Experience of Value*

Although a non-believer may admire and wish to emulate his Christian friend, if this Christian does not "reveal" to him the meaning of his experience, if no one ever speaks to him about anything except humanistic values, his admiration alone will not enable him to appreciate the faith or give him reasons for entering the Church.

It is true that the content of faith is not man-made. Through what Paul calls "preaching," a "revelation" must take place (Rom. 10:14–17). Nonetheless, today in a pluralistic culture only a discriminating experience of value

[27] Some will claim that if the norm for adhesion to the Church is an experience of value, there is no hope. Although some young people do no doubt experience valid groups within the Church, on the whole most do not and, in that case, they are bound to lose the faith. We disagree. Such assertions unintentionally spread panic. Given the human condition, we don't think that the Church—if put on the same plane —is any worse than Marxism or any other movement. We think that globally it even gives a powerful witness; otherwise it would be defeated and this would prove definitely that Christ is dead. And yet, this witness, if it is to be concretely shown, presupposes the grace of faith, as well as response to this grace.

is likely to lead to a conscious, free faith; all other norms will be either ineffective or inadequate.[28]

PRINCIPLES FOR EDUCATING

How can we educate young people to appreciate value correctly, examine it critically and understand it more fully in relation to the Word of God?

1. *Sharing Their Search*

Formerly the religion teacher began with his own questions, or standard ones, and responded with standard answers. Thus, the question, "Why should I confess to a priest and not directly to God?" yielded the response that the grace of God is communicated to men through signs. Whether he liked it or not, the young person had to be satisfied with this method; his traditional world sustained him and encouraged him to be faithful.

Today the starting point should not be a set of standard

---

[28] Some will object that many young people choose the Church not because they have experienced the goodness or truth of some doctrine, but because they feel comfortable with a certain group of Christians whose ways of thinking, loving and behaving they spontaneously adopt. This is true enough, but it only confirms our contention earlier that participation in a group resolves problems of meaning. The basic issue remains constant: the group is chosen according to an experience of value.

questions but the acceptance of pluralism. The tension between various opinions is, in fact, the real issue. In addition, having agreed to this issue, we must accompany our young people on their quest for meaning, and be truly open to the varied ways in which different ages and religions have answered the question of faith. Most important, this quest must be honest and objective. We should not clothe the thought of the unbeliever in the trappings of faith but rather put ourselves in his shoes and try to understand his position as *he* states it.

Through joining in this search we are continuing the Incarnation. By presuming that each of the various solutions found by men has its own appeal and power to raise questions, we shall make Christ concretely present to the fact of pluralism. By confronting with young people the contradictions and richnesses of diverse perspectives, we shall bring Emmanuel, "God with us" into this historical and cultural environment.

2. *Deepening the Search*

We can enlarge the dimensions of the search in two ways: first, through material which can open, challenge, broaden the search; and second, through questions and projects which can deepen it.

When young people return from field trips and projects, and meet in small groups with proposals, ideas and solutions, they have already begun to make choices. To develop these choices and enlarge their significance without bruising them by authoritarian intrusion, teachers need to cultivate the art of questioning. On the one hand they should ask questions about ultimate meanings which young people, because of their existential sensibility, often overlook; and on the other hand, they should ask functional questions. Although we must not lose sight of the fact that many of our pragmatic contemporaries are not interested in abstract debate and absolute questions, we can explore the possibilities of raising functional questions in such a way as to include ultimate issues. The psychological question of man's optimal functioning and the fulfillment of his highest needs, for instance, can be considered a pragmatic question of ultimate meaning.

Take, for example, the position of most young people in favor of birth control. Certain basic questions about why they feel this way can help them grasp the value—in this case, love—and these can be questions of function: Can birth control improve one's capacity to love? Is there any risk of just using one another for egoistic pleasure? What does it mean to have children? How would we raise children? How does love mature?

3. Presenting Faith as Faith

Two points must be stressed: faith must be proposed, not imposed; faith must be proposed as faith, not ideology.

Proposing faith. Karl Barth describes the conditions for presenting faith to our time as follows: "Our fathers and grandfathers understood the gospel as a law of faith and of morality. We perhaps have been given the chance to realize that the gospel message is a message of freedom. Not 'You must believe,' but 'You have permission to believe.' "[29]

And Pope Paul in the encyclical *Ecclesiam Suam* stresses that "the dialogue of salvation does not force anyone to receive it; it is a formidable demand of love which, though it constitutes a serious responsibility for those it addresses, nonetheless leaves them free to answer or refuse."[30]

This point is crucial. In a traditional society faith could be mixed up with overall systems of thought; today, however, a distinction must be made. We need not fear this; on the contrary, in such a situation faith can emerge all the more purely. Our response to questions will not be "Here is the Truth and the Truth is Christ," or "Here is the solution in Christ"; such answers are untrue to our pluralistic reality. They abruptly destroy the integrity of sincere discussion by introducing a transcendent element which is always right and beyond debate because it comes from heaven. Although we should not deny the truth of Christ, we must not violate the truth of dialogue either. The only way out of this dilemma is to represent faith as the faith of Christians, and not as truth in itself. Instead of claiming "Here is the Truth

[29] *I.C.I.* 266 (Aug. 15, 1966).
[30] On faith as proposal, without constraint or pressure, see "Declaration on Religious Liberty," No. 11.

and the Truth is Christ," we should say "Christians think" or "we believe that . . ." This will situate Christ in his proper place within the discussion. He is not an element discussible on the same level as an ideology. He is an object of faith, hence, a reality that is believed, and not a system which demands acceptance because of its coherence.

Presenting faith as other than ideology. Although we present faith as "what Christians believe," we need not fear that we are thereby reducing faith to the status of one more cultural option. Behind the ideologies evolved by Christians stands this great reality, Christ, who reveals God to man. He is the Son: "No one has ever seen God; the only begotten Son who is in the Father's bosom has made him known" (Jn. 1:18; cf. Matt. 11:27). He does this by constantly referring us to another on whom he depends and from whom he receives everything: the Father. Isn't this how John shows us the divinity of Jesus? "I do not speak of myself but the Father who has sent me, he tells me what I am to say" (Jn. 12:49; cf. 7:16–17, 17:7–8).

The apostles in turn received everything from Christ. They did not speak of themselves but, filled with the Spirit, proclaimed Christ (Acts 4:19–20; 5:29–32; 1 Jn. 1:1–3). Christ is at the center of apostolic preaching which refers men to the event and the fact of his death and resurrection. Because the apostles are witnesses and not authors of this event, Christianity is not merely an ideology. Its originality resides in the fact that Christ was witness of the Father and

63

the apostles in turn witnessed to Someone who worked with them and confirmed the Word.

The pluralistic approach to this material should not cause the teacher to efface himself when he speaks of Christ; rather he should speak, not of truths he possesses or dogmas he carries in his pocket, but of *one who infinitely surpasses him.* Only in this way can catechesis be stripped of its authoritarianism while, at the same time, its greatest appeal is manifested.

Here the teacher's own faith and attitude are decisive factors. Biblical references, Council documents, and theological reflections are all in danger of remaining dead letters unless they are underlined by the faith of the teacher himself and by the attitude of a man who depends on Jesus Christ. Instead of locking students into one teacher's approach, catechesis should lead them into silent dialogue with the Other. In short, we must pass from authoritarian indoctrination or a dialectic of proof to a dialectic of sign. The convincing factor in the presentation of faith will not be argumentative power but gentleness and discretion, serenity, and humility.

4. *Providing Objective Guarantees for Group Experience*

The risk of using experiential value as an essential norm is that of becoming imprisoned in a limited and distorted subjectivity. We dare not underestimate this danger. Nothing constrains as much as pure subjectivity. Is it possible for a young person caught up in the emotions of a first love to doubt the goodness of premarital sex? Granted that some of the traditional answers retain a validity, how can we respond to him on the level of experiential value?

The only way to help young people avoid the imprisonment of inadequate subjective experience is to provide objective norms and guarantees *with reference to the group* and *to history*. The group is the overall individual expanded, criticized, and opened to the universal. History is a guide to the most constant, most valid direction of the total human community. If young people want to be true to the experience of value, they must be willing to go all the way, so that their experience is somehow linked to the total experience of humanity before and around them. This will not only safeguard and broaden them; it will also help all men advance in the search for truth.

Take, for example, this problem of premarital sex relations. We can question its validity in regard to love or as a preparation for marriage, its possibly egoistic motivation, its capacity to bring personal happiness. But we can also question its implications for society as a whole: How does it affect the whole institution of marriage? What about venereal disease? If we admit that lust ends in emptiness and ennui, how can we be assured that premarital sex will not end in culture-wide lust?

We would not want to discourage new initiatives weighty with consequences for morality or religion, but we do have the right—and teenagers accept this—to ask questions; What are the consequences for those around you of your leaving a certain commitment or group; of your choosing certain moral orientations? Is your choice a subjective whim or the result of careful reflection? Have you seen your alternatives simply as "staying" or "leaving," overlooking the possibility of staying and working with others to rebuild and renew the group?

The immediate context of these questions of experiential value should not be an imposed group but a voluntary community. Although at the beginning a group of friends is usually more or less given, they should gradually be consciously chosen. Christians will consider contact with the Christian community and its ministers crucial to their faith, and non-Christians will choose another mode of belonging to a group.

Ultimately what really matters is that young people accept their desire for belonging as their only chance of growing to a fulfillment of understanding and love. The person who separates himself, goes it alone, will lose himself from the advance of humanity. From the Christian perspective, refusal to participate in the Christian community cuts off one's chance of being open to the humanity and divinity revealed in Jesus Christ.

Most young people will accept this principle of objectification through the group. It is, in fact, the only such form of control they can accept in a world which refuses any monolithic ideology. Not that this belonging is easy—far from it. But it is true to their concrete, pragmatic, historical mode of apprehension and it is in line with their social orientation.

Pluralism implies coping with one's own existence without losing touch with everyone else's.[31]

---

[31] Some people may feel that these ideas are naive, that given so much freedom of choice and few sanctions, teenagers will inevitably choose "the easy way out," the most selfish course of action. We would argue that this approach is not the result of naiveté but of an optimistic belief in the ultimate attractiveness of Christ, and in the capacity of young people to respond to him, even without the authoritarian safeguards of traditional cultures.

II.

SECOND OBJECTIVE:
THE EXPERIENCE OF LOVE

Although it may seem strange at first to propose such an objective in a course on the Church, it is nonetheless essential, both doctrinally and psychologically.

DOCTRINALLY

What in fact is the Church? What can be said about it that really matters? Precisely this: that somewhere in this world there exists an "assembly of brothers" to whom the Revelation of God's infinite love for man has been made. The Church is nothing else than the historical, permanent witness of the "God who has so loved the world . . ." The essence of the Church is to know the Father's measureless love and to manifest it to the world. All else—its institutions, sacraments, hierarchy, canon law—exists meaningfully only to proclaim and help men live according to this Revelation.

The catechesis of the Church consequently has as its goal, in words and in actions, the "revelation" of love. It must transmit the basic experience of the first disciples whose hands touched the Word of Life: they knew love because God loved them first. All our explanations must revolve around this central perspective of love. Furthermore, if it is true that experiential value is the norm of choice, what other experience is more likely to open men to an understanding of the Church than the experience of love: "Love alone is worthy of faith," writes Urs von Balthasar.

All young people beginning to love know this very well. More important for their deepest acceptance than the intellectual caliber of the teacher is the sincerity with which they love and feel loved. They will come to the Church through love, not reason. Therefore, if the Church offers no love, none of love's freedom and élan, they will join another club. And we will have nothing to say to them.

PSYCHOLOGICALLY

Beyond doctrinal considerations, love is called for by the state of our times. The chief complaint of this century seems to be a "sickness of the heart." Hippies rejecting order for the sake of loving freely, the "sex revolution," the popularity of sentimental movies, TV shows, and magazines all indicate this need for love. Men of traditional societies suffer this less, because in rural civilizations human proximity, parental ties, a unity of customs and habits make possible organic fulfillment of emotional needs. Contemporary civilization on the other hand has exploded: most men are transient, overwhelmed by work, caught up in a huge, collective whirl. We are far from the hearth and the village. Abruptly, brutally seized by social change, man suffers from a scattering of himself. Anxious evasion, revolt, frantic activity, hedonism are poor compensations for acute emptiness.

More than ever before, young people need to be recreated by love. Proof of this is provided by the success of teachers who are not only intellectually competent and dynamic, but also generous and loving.

That the Church may be a "temptation." The "miracle" of John XXIII was that God's love for the world became visible in him. As the Swiss theologian Zundel put it, "In him truth and love were never separated."

We cannot indicate all the conditions for such an education of love. Group life, common leisure, unlimited commitment, concern for the "underdog," forgiveness granted "70 times 7" have all been mentioned frequently in religious education manuals, and belong in a catechisis of the Church. What chiefly prevents full commitment to the Church is its formalism, legalism, and dogmatism.[32]

What a "temptation" the Church would be if it were first of all the community of those who live this love and proclaim it to the world!

---

[32] These are flaws which indicate a rejection of the original vital adventure of Love: in all pharisaism the freshness of the Spirit is replaced by stereotypes, stiffening forms, refusal to lose oneself, and fidelity to the letter only.

III.

THIRD OBJECTIVE:
DIALOGUE AND SOLIDARITY
WITH ALL MEN

This too follows from our understanding of the world which is coming to be.

How do we avoid deception? There is no way of knowing what the Church of tomorrow—the forms of Christian life and Church participation, the credentials of a Christian—will be like. Yet it hardly seems prophetic to predict that present forms defining Church membership will disappear. The "good Catholic" will no longer be identified by attendance at Sunday Mass, Catholic schooling, participation in Church projects.

Given this prospect can we educate young people for a goal that will not deceive them, that will be able to undergo all the mutations of form, all the interplanetary journeys, all the social upheavals ahead of us? We can return to the essentials and take up that book which is never out of date: "By this shall all men know you, that you love one another."

These words transcend history. Fraternal charity under the inspiration of divine charity is the essence of Christianity, of that religious spirit and truth which will not pass away. What, then, are the most significant expressions of love in our time? What will be the most tangible sign of the love of Christ today? Each of us, no doubt, must answer for himself according to his own charism. But generally we can characterize the forms of charity in two ways: dialogue and international solidarity. Since solidarity often takes the form of dialogue, the two go together.

DIALOGUE

"This is an attitude which the Catholic Church must adopt in this moment of the world's history . . . With regard to that inner drive of love which tends to translate itself into an external gift, we shall use the name customary today, dialogue. The Church must enter into dialogue with the world . . . She must become word, message, conversation."[33]

The characteristic of Christian holiness in polycultural societies is dialogue. If the charity of traditional societies was often expressed through fervent defense of the forms of the ancient patrimony, the charity of pluralistic societies expresses itself primarily in the desire to meet, with infinite respect and unconditional sympathy, the other.[34]

---

[33] Paul VI, *Ecclesiam Suam, I.C.I.* (Sept. 1, 1964), pp. 12–13).

[34] This does not of course mean relinquishing dogma but it does suggest another way of presenting it. (This point is not fully developed here because it is treated in *Options* [Pierre Babin, New York, 1967].)

INTERNATIONAL SOLIDARITY

This means solidarity with all peoples as well as with all churches. Can we capitalize on the opportunity offered by the world's irreversible movement toward internationalization? Will we know how to decipher the possibility in this movement of realizing the law of universal love?

"A new commandment I give you: love one another as I have loved you—love your enemies—proclaim the gospel to every creature." This commandment must be translated historically into the desire to break through racial and nationalistic barriers, to share wealth on a worldwide scale (hence to understand the needs of others), to encounter all religions, and come to harmony with all quests for transcendent value.

Whereas traditional man turned to the past for guidance, modern man spontaneously turns toward the future, with science as his guide. The modern Christian seeks a solid progress which is not simply the outcome of scientific planning, but rather of defining an evangelical lifestyle based on understanding the signs of the times. Dialogue, openness to the universe and solidarity with all men constitute such a Christian becoming and outline a future that is solidly built on essentials.

If the catechesis of the Church produces a man who is more dogmatic, rather than one who is open to universal brotherhood, we will have tragically missed the signs of the times.

73

IV.

FOURTH OBJECTIVE:
A SENCE OF MISSION

WHY THIS OBJECTIVE?

The basic questions of young Christians today, problems which cultural pluralism and the affluent society make more urgent than ever before, can perhaps be reduced to three:

(1) Does God exist? (We get along fine without him.)

(2) Is the Church really the source of Christ, the place where he is experienced and recognized? (If not, why bother with it? We'd rather reach Christ without having to pass through that structure.)

(3) What is the purpose in my being a Christian, in my belonging to the Church?

Our last objective will answer the third of these, a crucial question:

Theologians have told us over and over again for at least thirty years that one can be saved without explicitly belonging to the "Bark of Peter" and that the goal of going to Church is not to pay one's fare to heaven. If so, young people say, then why bother with the Church? Formerly to belong to the Church was the "thing to do," through conformity or social tradition at least: the Church was for our ancestors a safe, normal socio-cultural power. But why remain in this "enclosed garden" when a thousand other forms of participation and identity—often more exciting than those offered by the Church—are available?

ONE SINGLE ANSWER

The point of belonging to the Church is simply this: We are not in the Church for ourselves but for others. The Church is not meant to refurbish herself but to serve the world so that all may attain to fullness of light and life.

"The test of the Council's success," said Msgr. de Provenchere, Archbishop of Aix, "is the missionary renewal of the Church." This was the great direction taken in the discussions and texts of Vatican II, and it is the basic orientation in this presentation of the Church. We are less concerned with the Church's nature in itself or in relation to God alone than with the Church in relation to the gospel which must be revealed to the world. We shall define the Church by its mission, and we shall invite young people to enter the Church through their own sense of the personal, specific mission they are to fulfill.

As experience shows, there are two kinds of Christians: those for whom the Church is a self-service, who take what they please; and those for whom the Church is "sole salvation for the world," who truly have the Church's interest at heart and who exist in the Church as they exist in their bodies. Such Christians identify with the Church[35] because they have a sense of mission as a result of their belonging to it. In other words, to refer back to Friedman's analysis, these Christians have solved within the Church their needs for identity and participation: They know themselves to be recognized in the highest possible way by the call of the Lord; and they are aware of participating, of playing an essential role in a great enterprise.

Without this consciousness of mission, belonging to the Church can remain ambiguous or childish in this pluralistic world which demands so much awareness and decision. We must make sure that doctrinal reflections do not lead to a pseudo-beatitude of thought or a "spiritual life" cut off from the world, but rather to a sense of mission which is open to universal meanings and willing to express itself in sacrifice "in order to gather into one the children of God who are dispersed."

These then are our objectives in educating young people about the Church.

---

[35] That is, they do not speak of the Church as a society outside themselves. (The way we speak of the Church is often a measure of our belonging: is it "us"? "they"? "the priests"? "the system"?)

PART THREE

METHOD

METHOD

I.

WHAT IS OUR METHOD AND WHY?

The method we must use to attain these educational objectives seems perhaps too risky: starting with an explosive issue, inviting the most diverse responses to it, some even contradictory, and then allowing the students to discover their own truths. This seems indeed a complete rejection of traditional catechesis. The dangers of religious relativism and of a total lack of structure seem all too evident. Why should we naïvely add to the heap of objections already stored in their heads? In the long run, what right do we have to deprive these young people of the very transmission of truth they are seeking, whether they know it or not?

These are certainly valid questions. We must take them into consideration if we are to avoid failure. And yet we still choose, quite deliberately, the method of greater openness —for two reasons:

(1) We have no right to evade the issue of pluralism;

(2) Pluralism has its positive as well as its negative aspects.

1. *We Can Not Avoid What Is a Real Problem*

Pluralism is a fact. It is a situation in which young people find themselves every day. At the age of fourteen, they come to class and ask about "free love"; they want to know more about Charles Davis leaving the Church; they have already taken stands on clerical celibacy; they accuse Rome of obscurantism for denying permission for Jazz Masses. Girls from Catholic schools want to know why they can't go to communion with Protestants; "Why can't we consider the Church as a self-service; we'll take what we please and leave the rest—the stale stuff—behind."

These are the facts. We may deplore them, but we can't evade them. Mass culture passes them on, universally imposes them, and creates, despite all opposition, a common identity among young people scattered throughout our towns and cities.

What should we do? Wear blindfolds and earplugs? Brandish the banners of truth and thunder around in the armor of authority?

The sincere teacher cannot, of course, resort to such theatrics, no matter how worried he might be about things falling apart or about insoluble dilemmas. He realizes that if he does not face the situation squarely, he will be un-faithful to Christ and to the young people he loves. He knows too that a faith which today has to lean on authori-tarianism and abstractions will collapse tomorrow under the pressure of cultural change.

Naturally an educator is not going to search foolishly for ways to multiply insoluble problems; but if he is to reach his students, he must encourage them to ask whatever ques-tions are real for them, however prying, impertinent or personal they seem. Rather than turn deaf ears to such questions, he should, if necessary, admit that he doesn't have the answers. An educator with "all the answers" can be far more destructive than the one who acknowledges his own limitations and searches with his students. The teacher who has an answer for everything can force his students into either complacent stasis or a complete rejection of him and all his answers.

There will never be a time when most students accept answers for everything, when they cease to question dogma and morality, but they might be better off tomorrow, better prepared to continue their quest, if the teacher has shared his search with them. They might even be closer to truth because of the witness of one who *seeks* God rather than one who *possesses* him.

It is in such a spirit that we have written this, aware of the risks certainly, but even more aware that if we do not run these risks, no one will be left in the Church but choir boys and fanatics.

81

2. *Seizing the Opportunities of Pluralism*

Despite the risks, this method of greater openness allows us to make the most of the positive aspects of pluralism. Faith, by its nature, involves risks—but at its core is the ability to recognize the extraordinary potential of each situation and to allow this potential to triumph by placing Christ's all-powerful love at the center of the difficulties.

The first opportunity pluralism offers is the *growth of personal freedom.* Our age is the first to receive the chance discussed by Karl Barth; we have been given at last, *"permission* to believe." The risk which God himself has taken now becomes, with the dismissal of monolithic traditions, vast in its implications. To fear the new man who owes his liberation to polycultural society could be construed as a refusal to go along with God in this, his own creative and saving action.

Each man today, far more than in traditional societies, is faced with immediate decisions about good and evil. More than ever before, each person must question, evaluate, and choose for himself. Surely such a challenge to conscience and such a demand on personal freedom adds to the glory of God.

If we are to give personal freedom its full value, we must of course permit the widest variety of responses. Under such conditions it is more than likely that not all the students will arrive at the same conclusions or accept the exact meanings proposed by the teacher. A genuine experience of pluralism presupposes mutual respect; it does not imply that one or the other must be "converted." Pluralism precludes inquisitions.

Because of his position, the teacher often must bend over backwards to avoid imposing his own beliefs. He must be aware of the many subtle influences of his power as an authority figure and sometimes he has to go out of his way to create an atmosphere in which his students are genuinely free to make their own decisions. He does so of course because he values the fact of their free choice more than he values what he thinks the content of that choice should be, and because he respects their integrity as individuals more than he desires to spread his own convictions.

His reluctance to interfere with that choice does not mean however that he should back down on what he personally believes. His standing firm is as much a part of their experience of pluralism as the students' refusal to be threatened by his position. Even the student who steadfastly denies the appeal of Christianity should at least experience in this the reality of pluralism—if he learns to live with the teacher and to accept the fact that the teacher is a Christian and will keep on being a Christian whether the student is one or not. This learning to live pluralistically is in itself a Christian project because it is learning to live in love, with all the divisions and differences of perspective real love must bridge.

Furthermore it is quite possible that if a teacher is successful in teaching this experience of pluralism, he can leave the door open for another Christian to bring Christ to that student who, for the time being, rejects Christianity. If instead the student were presented with a standard dogmatic course on the Church, he might well resent it and develop such a thorough hatred for the Church that the door will be shut permanently. Not only will such a teacher lose this student; he is likely to lose the sympathy of other students who might share his beliefs but who resent his forcing them on the non-believer. We know how quickly allegiances within a classroom can shift if students sense that one of their own, especially an underdog, is being "persecuted" by the authority. If there is one universal allergy among young people today, it is the one towards authoritarianism and towards any use of power they regard as unfair. And whether or not such a teacher loses their sympathy, he will surely have lost the chance to show them the potential within pluralism for mutual respect.

The tensions of teaching pluralism within a course on the Church are especially complex in the case of nonbelievers who once belonged to the Church. We have sometimes been more willing to defend the rights of Hindus to believe what they believe than the rights of ex-Christians not to believe what *we* believe. The faith of the Hindu is of course far less threatening to our own because it does not usually represent a conscious choice about the same material. We are, furthermore, conditioned to regard ex-Catholics as apostates, heretics, sinners who have willfully refused the grace of God, after receiving all the opportunities: proper instruction, baptism, the gift of faith. It is much easier to tolerate the nonbelief of the Jewish agnostic or the different belief of the Moslem than to forgive the rejection of our own faith. We are only now—because of the splits among ourselves—seeing the full implications of what real Christian brotherhood requires.

If we are to go all the way in accepting and teaching pluralism we have to include not just the Hindu and the Jew but also the baptized student in front of us. One of the implications of our teaching this course on the Church is the possibility that this young believer could, while growing in personal consciousness and freedom, become a nonbeliever. We have to realize that coming to mature, responsible faith is so mysterious and individual a process that to force it upon students, however gently, is simply not God's way. Some people have obstructions in their experience which will always block the flowering of faith; others come to faith by such devious routes that a religion teacher can only stand back in awe. So we should know before we start that even when we *show* them Christianity—since a good teacher knows he can't just *tell* them about it—some students will not be able to respond, however impressed they may be. We must not respect them any less for this, which might be for them at this time a better decision, if for no other reason than that it is the authentic exercise of their personal freedom.

The second opportunity provided by pluralism is the *richness of perspectives* which can universalize our faith, make it more "catholic." Thanks to pluralism, whether we like it or not, the voices of the entire world and of all religions enter the Church, resound through its often narrow walls and stretch it far beyond its provincial horizons. In addition to giving us a sense of the universal Church, pluralism opens the road to international solidarity. Pluralism forces us to admit the validity of other perspectives—the alternative often being war—and once we have granted that, opens us to the incredible riches of approaches not our own. Rather than pretending that any one man or nation or religion has a complete monopoly on the truth, pluralism assumes that the truth is more available to all if it is approached through the sharing of a variety of viewpoints.

Today in our schools we see a healthy peaceful coexistence; young people of every background and belief live for the most part side by side without hostility. Tolerance is an accepted mode of response, but with it often is a great mutual indifference. With this peaceful coexistence as a base, pluralism offers us the chance to turn this indifference into openness so that each person, instead of ignoring the others, calls forth their special contributions. From now on, it should be impossible for any of us to exist, search, struggle without others. Together we are the many facets of a large, luminous crystal; apart we are merely splinters. Despite its risks—ideological indifference, total relativism—pluralism offers the incentive to grow still further. This growth emerges from the quality of exchange made possible today by freedom and equality in human relations.

In view of these possibilities, it is important for the teacher to relate issues crucial for young people to issues of import for the whole world. This is not to minimize the authenticity of student concerns but to put them into perspective and to prevent the students from entering so exclusively on their own problems that the issues become self-enclosed. One should not discuss birth control, for example, without reference to such problems as overpopulation and starvation. However remote they may seem for young people, these wider implications must become part of their consciousness.

This urgent task of opening individual problems to worldwide issues is made easier for the teacher by today's global communications through which every kind of particular explodes in a thousand directions, and such issues as war, discrimination, and economic crisis are so juxtaposed that one can scarcely ignore the interrelatedness of events. The task is not of course to make young people distinguish their problems from those of the world around them—and thus either concentrate solely on their own subjectivity or dismiss it as irrelevant—but to encourage them to work for breadth of insight and for communication with others.

II.

WHAT KIND OF PERSON ARE WE STRIVING FOR?

In order to educate, to "lead out," one needs some intuition of what is possible in the person he educates. A teacher is not really one who solves problems; rather he is one with a special insight into the *potential* man. This special insight has its source in love. By loving someone we see what he can become; our task as teachers is to make him more conscious of this, and thus help him become it.

To specify our vision of the potential man by some abstract portrait could be dangerous, if it prompted us unconsciously to lead our students out of their own uniqueness into this box of perfection. Because we believe in the basic goodness of each individual, we can risk the goal of allowing each person to come to his own fulfillment, whether or not it fits our predictions or satisfies our own aspirations.

At the same time, we obviously hope that each person's fulfillment will make him more loving, more committed to his own positive action in the world, and more aware of the struggles of the rest of mankind. We would like to create for him, first, an atmosphere of freedom, in which his choices are genuine and his responsiveness integral to his own identity; out of this integrity we hope he will be able to discover a significance in life which will put him in profound touch with others and open him—without threat and without diminishment of commitment on anyone's part —to what is meaningful for all men; and finally, out of this openness we hope he can come to a mature, deeply grounded faith in Jesus Christ.

Such hopes may seem grandiose, such ideals self-defeating, but unless we have such far-reaching trust in the potential of those we educate, we can too easily become bogged down in the difficulties of reaching our students on the mere levels of subject matter or superficial adherence. If, for example, students distorted the doctrine of papal infallibility in a course on the Church, the teacher could feel the course was a waste of time. Or if they rejected the Church itself, we might easily consider this course a failure. But if our goals are based on the growth of their consciousness and the discovery of their integrity, we could never so nearly measure the success or failure of our efforts. Acknowledging that our own capacities to love are limited and that our encounter with any one student is only part of the larger educative process of his life, we could nonetheless trust with some certainty that this educative experience had been a positive one. Paradoxically then, the deeper, more extensive our goal, the greater our chance of reaching it.